Story of the Earth

Stuart Malin

Troll Associates

Library of Congress Cataloging-in-Publication Data

Malin, Stuart, (date)
   Story of the earth / by Stuart Malin.
     p.   cm.—(Exploring the universe)
   Summary: Describes the earth's birth, life forms, air, water,
seasons, moving continents, interior, and future.
   ISBN 0-8167-2134-3 (lib. bdg.)   ISBN 0-8167-2135-1 (pbk.)
   1. Earth—Juvenile literature. [1. Earth.] I. Title.
  II. Series.
  QB631.4.M35   1991
  550—dc20   90-11019

Published by Troll Associates

Edited by Neil Morris
Design by Sally Boothroyd
Picture research by Karen Gunnell

Printed in the U.S.A.

10 9 8 7 6 5 4 3 2 1

Illustrations:
Julian Baum cover, pp 6-7, 8-9, 12, 17, 18, 26
Rhoda & Robert Burns/Drawing Attention pp 4, 14 (top),
   22
Julie Douglas pp 14 (bottom), 25 (bottom)
Hans Jensen pp 10-11, 25 (top)

Picture credits:
Anglo-Australian Telescope Board pp 4-5
British Museum (Natural History) p 21
Bruce Coleman pp 10, 20-21, 31 (bottom)
Mark Edwards/Still Pictures p 28
European Space Agency p 1
Akira Fujii pp 2-3
Geoscience Features p 27 (bottom)
Hutchison p 19
Frank Lane pp 15, 28-29, 31 (top)
NASA pp 12, 13
Royal Observatory Edinburgh p 7
Frank Spooner p 24
ZEFA back cover, pp 16, 18-19, 23, 27 (top), 29, 30

Front cover: the young, hot, mostly molten Earth.
Back cover: Yosemite National Park, California, USA.
Title page: Earth from space.
Pages 2-3: the constellation of Sagittarius.

Contents

Where are we?

Have you ever written out your *full* address, ending Earth, Solar System, Milky Way Galaxy, the Universe? When the intergalactic mail carrier comes to deliver a letter, he or she will first have to pick out our galaxy, or cluster of stars, from the millions of similar ones dotted about in space. Having found it, the mail carrier will have to hunt through the 100,000 million stars that make up the Galaxy until he or she finds the rather ordinary star that we call the Sun.

▶ The spiral galaxy NGC 2997. This is roughly how our galaxy would look if we could see it from the outside, with the solar system in one of the clouds of stars toward the edge.

▼ The solar system consists of the Sun, nine planets and their moons, and small bits of debris.

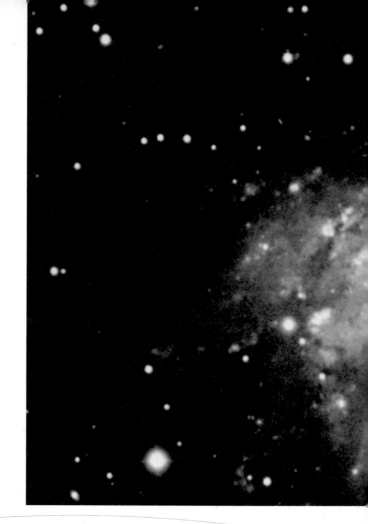

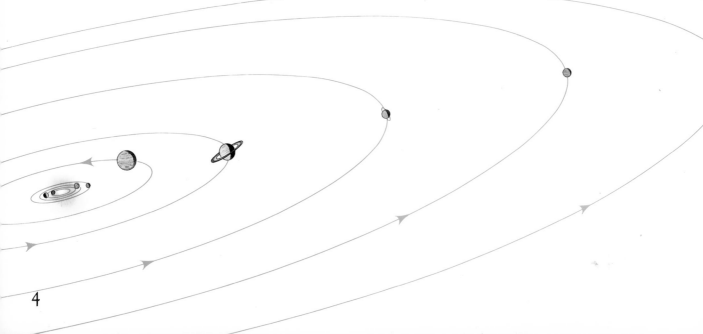

What is special about the Sun is that it has nine planets going around it. The planets would not be easy for the mail carrier to see from a distance, because they are tiny compared to the Sun and, unlike stars, they give out no light of their own. They show up only because they reflect sunlight.

By far the largest of the planets is Jupiter, though it is still only one-thousandth the volume of the Sun. Between the Sun and Jupiter there are four small rocky planets. The third one from the Sun, after Mercury and Venus, is the Earth. The mail carrier would have no difficulty in recognizing it, because it has a large Moon going around it. Mars, the fourth planet, has two moons, but they are both very small. Venus and Mercury have none.

So this is where we live, on a small planet orbiting, or circling around, an ordinary star near the edge of an equally ordinary galaxy surrounded by cold, dark, empty space. Don't forget to add your intergalactic zip code!

The birth of the solar system

Fifteen thousand million years ago, according to scientific theory, the universe came into existence with a huge explosion, much more violent than any that has happened since. At this first instant of creation, everything in the universe was packed together at a single point, but the explosion blew it apart and the universe is still spreading out.

After about a million years, space was filled with a thin cloud of expanding gas. Gradually the gas broke up and formed millions of separate clouds with empty space in between. Each of these clouds was a galaxy. Within each galaxy, over a long period of time, much the same process happened again, with the cloud of gas forming into separate cloudlets, each of which became a star.

Scientists say that is how the Sun was formed, about 4,600 million years ago. A gently rotating cloud of gas got pulled together by a force we call gravity and formed itself into a much smaller ball.

▶ This is how the universe might have looked just after it came into existence. Of course, there was no one around to see it, and there was absolutely nothing "outside." Also, the picture must have changed completely in a small fraction of a second.

As it did, two important things happened. First, the ball got hotter and hotter until at last it became a proper star, generating its energy in the same way as a hydrogen bomb. Secondly, some of the gas and dust left behind as the ball shrank collected together to form the planets.

The planets, too, got very hot as they formed, but they were not big enough to become stars, so they have now cooled down and get nearly all their heat and light from the Sun.

▼ The Pleiades is a group of very young stars that have only recently formed. They are still surrounded by the remains of the gas clouds from which they formed.

The early Earth

Like the other planets, the Earth formed as a collection of debris left behind by the contracting Sun. Scientists theorize that as each new fragment of debris crashed onto the forming planet, it made the Earth a little hotter, until it became a red-hot, semi-molten ball. The heavier material sank toward the middle, and a lighter "scum" worked its way up to the surface. It was much too hot for there to be any oceans, of course, but there was a thick atmosphere, or layer of gases, above the surface. Much of this original atmosphere, particularly the lighter gases in it, such as hydrogen, got swept away by the stream of fast-moving particles that poured out from the Sun.

▲ The Earth started as a cloud of gas, rocks, and dust. It lost much of its gas to become a hot, spherical planet. When it had collected most of the nearby material, it cooled down and solidified.

▶ When the Earth was young, it was very hot and almost molten. The surface may have looked like this, with clouds of gas and dust blocking out much of the sunlight. Illumination came from great plumes of glowing molten rock and pools.

8

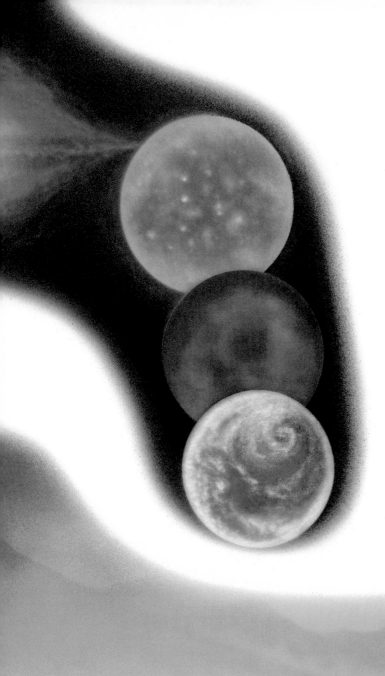

As the Earth cooled, it started to solidify from the surface down, though deep inside it remains molten even today. The early surface was covered with volcanoes, spewing out vast quantities of dust, gas, and molten rock. When it was cool enough, the steam in the atmosphere condensed into water droplets, which fell as rain, washing much of the volcanic dust out of the atmosphere. The rain ran downhill in streams and rivers, and collected into huge pools, which eventually became the oceans.

But even with oceans and rivers, the Earth was quite unlike the planet we know today. There was no life of any sort, not so much as a single blade of grass, and the air was quite unbreathable because it contained hardly any oxygen.

Life on Earth

There is only one place in the universe where life is known, and that is on the planet Earth. Blue-green algae – one of the most primitive forms of life, like the slime that forms on stagnant pools – probably first appeared over 3,000 million years ago, when the Earth was a third its present age. Green algae, a slightly more advanced form of life, developed about 1,000 million years ago, and shellfish about 500 million years ago.

Plants and animals first appeared on land 400 million years ago, and it is only for the past two million years that anything recognizable as human has existed.

Now the planet is teeming with life: algae, seaweed, and fish in the sea; birds and insects in the air; and an incredible variety of fungus, plants, trees, and animals on the land. But it is the blue-green algae that made all this possible, not just because it came first, but because it started the process of releasing oxygen into the atmosphere, which is essential for almost every other form of life.

◀ Blue-green algae seen through a microscope (*top left*). Life on Earth has developed over hundreds of millions of years.

The view from space

What would the Earth look like to astronomers on the planet Mars? Without a telescope, they would see it as a bright point of light in the morning or evening sky. Through a telescope, the Earth would look to the astronomers on Mars very much as the Moon does to us: not always the same shape, but varying from a slim crescent to a full disk as it travels around the Sun. They would find out that the Earth takes exactly one year to circle the Sun, and that it takes the Moon 27⅓ days to complete its orbit, or path, around the Earth.

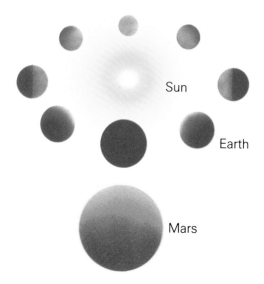

▲ The Sun can illuminate only the half of Earth that faces toward it. The rest is in darkness. From Mars, the Earth would appear to go through the same phases as our Moon does to us.

▼ The Earth photographed from space by Apollo 17 astronauts.

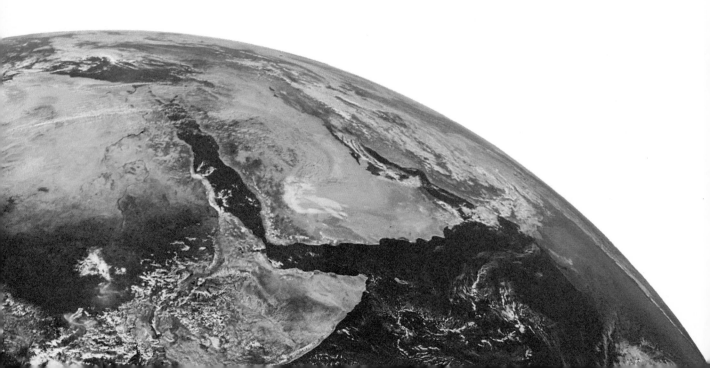

Much of the Earth is covered by white clouds, which change their shapes and positions. But looking between these, the Martian astronomers would see that there are markings on the surface – the continents and oceans – that keep the same shape but still appear to move. This is because the Earth is spinning, and the Martians might be surprised to discover that it rotates at about the same rate as their own planet, making a complete spin once a day or 365¼ times in a year.

Our Martian astronomers could learn all of this from their observations and quite a lot more. For example, they could measure the size and shape of the Earth.

They would find that it is almost spherical, with a diameter of about 8,000 miles. They could also work out the mass of the Earth, from the size of the Moon's orbit and the time the Moon takes to complete an orbit around the Earth. Mass is not the same as weight, because weight depends on gravity. But even in space, where there is no gravity and a body is weightless, it still has mass, as you would find out if it collided with you. They would discover that the Earth's mass is 6,600 million million million tons.

▼ This is how the Earth looked to astronauts in their lunar module above the Moon. They must have felt a very long way from home.

The seasons

The main reason for the differences of temperature throughout the year is the height of the Sun above the horizon. When the Sun is high in the sky, all the heat in a beam of sunlight falls on a small area that becomes quite hot. When the Sun is low in the sky, the same beam of sunlight is spread over a much larger area, which does not get so warm. This is why it is hotter in summer than winter.

Near the North and South Poles the Sun never gets high in the sky, so it is always cold. In fact, during the winter at the poles the Sun never gets above the horizon, so it is always night. This is made up for during the summer at the poles, when the Sun never sets.

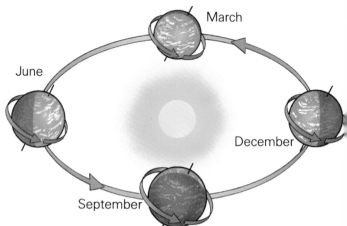

▼ The tilt of the Earth's axis gives us the seasons. In December the Northern Hemisphere is tilted away from the Sun and has long nights and short days. In June it is tilted towards the Sun and has long days and short nights.

March

June

December

September

But even then the Sun stays close to the horizon all day long, so the temperature still doesn't get very warm. In contrast, at the equator the Sun passes nearly overhead every day of the year, so it is very hot there.

◄ When a flashlight shines directly downward, it sheds a lot of light on a small area. When it shines at an angle, the same light covers a larger area, so the surface is less brightly lit. The same happens with the light and heat from the Sun.

► In summer, if you are north of the Arctic Circle it is always daylight. If the sky is clear, you can see the Sun above the horizon even at midnight. This photograph of the midnight Sun was taken in Norway.

Although the Earth is spinning freely in space and does not have an axle, the line where the axle would be if it had one is called the *axis of rotation*. It passes through the North and South Poles. The Earth's axis always points in the same direction in space, at an angle to the direction the Earth is traveling in as it goes around the Sun. For this reason, sometimes the North Pole is tilted a little toward the Sun, but when the Earth is on the other side of its orbit six months later, it is tilted away. When the North Pole is tilted toward the Sun, the Northern Hemisphere gets more sunlight, so this is the summer season there; but the Southern Hemisphere gets less sunlight, so it is winter there. Six months later the seasons are reversed, with winter in the north and summer in the south.

Air

The Earth is surrounded by the layer of air we call the atmosphere. It is a very thin layer – an aircraft cruising at 29,000 feet has more air below it than above it – but it is very important. Without it, there would be no rain, no weather, no life.

The atmosphere is made up of about four parts of nitrogen to one part of oxygen, with much smaller quantities of other gases. The oxygen is particularly useful to us because we need to breathe it to stay alive. Also, high up in the atmosphere, some of the oxygen changes into a special form called ozone, which provides a barrier to harmful radiation from the Sun.

Some of the other gases in the air are also important. Carbon dioxide (the same gas that forms bubbles in soft drinks) helps to control the temperature of the Earth, and water vapor forms the clouds. The atmosphere is a thin but very effective blanket that protects the Earth from outer space.

▶ An aircraft flying at about 29,000 feet is above nearly all the clouds and weather, and more than half the atmosphere. This does not mean that the atmosphere ends suddenly at 58,000 feet. It goes out much further than that, but it gets thinner and thinner as you go higher.

▼ Seen from above, clouds look like layers of absorbent cotton, but inside they are cold and damp, like mist or fog. They help to keep the heat out during the day, and warmth in at night.

None of the other planets has an atmosphere quite like that of the Earth. Mercury has hardly any atmosphere at all. Mars has an atmosphere a hundred times thinner than ours. Venus has a lot of carbon dioxide in its atmosphere. This lets the heat of the Sun come in, but does not let it out again, so the planet is very hot. Venus also has a complete cloud cover, so there is no future for astronomers there. The four giant planets – Jupiter, Saturn, Uranus, and Neptune – have atmospheres hundreds of miles thick, made up mainly of hydrogen, helium, and methane.

6 mi.

3 mi.

Water

Perhaps the most peculiar thing about the Earth is that so much of it is covered with water. Over seven tenths of the Earth's surface is ocean, with an average depth of about 2½ miles. When water freezes, it turns into ice, which is solid. And when it is heated above a certain temperature, it evaporates, or turns into an invisible vapor, or gas. Ice and water vapor are quite common in the outer planets, but it is only on the surface of the Earth that the temperature is right for water to exist in liquid form.

▼ The water cycle. Water rises from the sea as vapor, then condenses to form clouds. Water then falls as rain and returns to the sea.

◄ The Goosenecks of San Juan, Utah, USA. The San Juan river at the bottom of the gorge looks gentle enough, but it has carved out the whole of the gorge and is still making it deeper. It does this mainly by scraping the river bed with pebbles and grit that it is carrying to the sea.

▲ Mount Kilimanjaro, in Tanzania, is 19,340 feet high. At that height it is cold enough for snow to stay throughout the year, even though it is very close to the equator.

Water evaporates from the sea into the atmosphere, where it forms clouds and then falls as rain. But the level of the sea is almost constant, because the rain that falls over land collects into streams and rivers and returns to the sea. Rivers also carry salt to the sea, so the sea is gradually getting saltier.

Why is it that rivers nearly always reach the ocean at sea level, rather than by plunging over cliffs as waterfalls? The reason is that running water does not simply flow over the land, but wears it away, shaping the landscape as it does so. Even a small river can create a wide valley.

Around the poles and high up in the atmosphere, the temperature is cold, so in these regions most of the water is found as snow or ice. When a cloud is formed high enough up, it is made up of ice crystals, which sometimes fall as snow. In many parts of the world snow melts fairly quickly, but in cold regions like the Arctic and Antarctic, or on high mountains, it can last a very long time without thawing. Mount Kilimanjaro, the highest peak in Africa, is close to the equator, but it is high enough to have a permanent cap of snow.

The Earth's changing face

The appearance of the Earth is constantly changing. It is only because of our short lifespan that we do not notice the slow natural changes that happen over millions of years.

There are four main processes at work. The first of these is *weathering* – the breaking up of rocks into small pieces, or particles. Heat and cold are good at doing this. Then there are the effects of waves pounding away at the coastline and of rainwater dissolving salts out of rock. There are many such processes, all working together to break up the surface of the landscape.

The broken bits of rock do not stay where they are. They can be washed down by rain, and carried away by streams and rivers. Or they may be blown away by the wind, or simply fall down. These processes are called *transportation*, because they all move the rock particles from a higher place to a lower one, and eventually to the sea.

The third stage is *deposition*. Once the rock particles have reached the sea, they gradually sink to the bottom. There they form layers of mud that gradually get compressed as more and more bits of rock settle on top of them.

If these were the only processes at work, the landscape would eventually become totally flat – no hills, no mountains, just a huge plain. But the fourth process is *uplift*. Over millions of years, movements within the Earth can force up vast areas of sea bed to thousands of feet above sea level. Then weathering, transportation, and deposition start all over again. Even on the highest mountains, you sometimes find layers of rock that were once at the bottom of the sea and can see fossilized sea creatures embedded in them.

◀ Bryce Canyon, Utah, USA. This spectacular landscape has been formed by the natural processes of weathering and transportation, with wind playing a major part.

▼ These fossils are the remains of creatures that originally lived in the sea. When they died, the hard parts of their bodies were preserved in mud which turned into rock.

Moving continents

Have you noticed how closely the west coast of Africa matches the east coast of South America? If you were to cut out the continents to make jigsaw pieces, you could fit them together quite well, with Africa next to South America and Europe next to North America.

    This led the German scientist Alfred Wegener to suggest in 1912 that there was once a great continent that split up and drifted apart. The idea was too startling to be taken seriously at the time, but it would not go away. Studies of the Earth's magnetism, fossils, and the ancient climate all suggested the same thing. Nowadays it is possible to measure the tiny changes in the positions of continents, and these too suggest that Wegener was right.

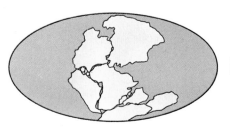  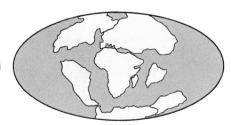

▲ Over the past 200 million years, the map of the world has changed dramatically. Originally just one deep ocean covered most of the globe. The rest was shallow sea or land. The land masses have since moved apart.

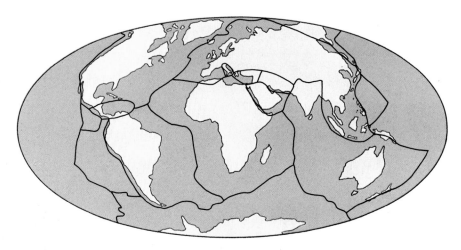

◄ The surface of the Earth is made up of a number of rigid plates that move about independently. Volcanoes and earthquakes occur near their boundaries.

► An erupting volcano is a magnificent sight, with molten rock and gas being forced out of a vent from a magma chamber below. The molten rock may flow out as lava, or be exploded out high into the air. This is Kilauea volcano, in Hawaii.

The "jigsaw pieces" that make up the Earth's surface are called *plates*. These slide about independently, though they move only a few inches each year. When plates rub against one another or collide, they build up a strain that is released as an earthquake. Or the plates squeeze rocks until they melt and erupt as volcanoes, or buckle up to make mountains. Volcanoes and earthquakes are quite different things, but they mostly happen at the edges of plates. By marking their positions on a map, we can see where the plate edges are.

Many of the large-scale features of the Earth can be understood in terms of plate movements. The Himalayas were formed when the Indian plate collided with the rest of Asia. The Atlantic is a region where two plates are moving apart, leaving a line of volcanoes down the middle of the ocean. The famous San Andreas Fault, the crack in the Earth's surface that runs through California, results from two plates sliding past one another. The deepest part of the world's oceans is where the Pacific plate dips down to slide under the Asian plate.

Earthquakes

Hardly a day goes by without an earthquake somewhere in the world. It is the release of the strain that has built up deep underground that makes the ground shake. The size of an earthquake depends on how much strain is released. Some earthquakes are so small they can be detected only with special instruments. Some sound and feel like a heavy truck passing by. But really large earthquakes, of which there are about two a year, can cause violent movements of the ground, with large cracks opening and closing, and destruction of buildings. A strong earthquake under the sea may produce a *tsunami*, or giant wave, which can cause great damage and loss of life when it reaches a shore.

How strong an earthquake feels depends on how close you are to the *epicenter*, or place where the strain is released. The effect gets weaker the further away you are, but many earthquakes can be detected even from the opposite side of the world by instruments called seismographs.

Vibrations spread out from the epicenter in all directions but they do not all travel at the same speed. The fastest moving are the P waves, so these are the first to reach a distant seismograph. The S waves are slower, so they lag further and further behind the P waves. By measuring the delay between the P and S waves, it is easy to work out how far away the epicenter is – since both types of waves start out together. With three well-separated seismographs, the exact position of the epicenter can be found, because there is only one point that is at the right distance from all three.

▶ The P, or primary, waves from an earthquake can be thought of as "push" waves, that move earth in the direction the wave is traveling. They work like a locomotive pushing freight cars. The locomotive pushes the first car, which then passes the push on to the next car, and so on, so that a "wave" appears to pass through the whole length of the train.

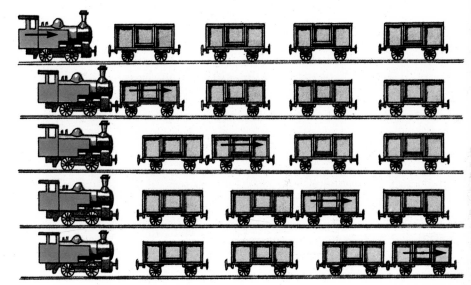

▶ The S, or secondary, waves can be thought of as "shake" waves. If you tie a piece of rope to a post and shake the free end up and down, an S wave will pass along the rope, but no part of the rope moves far from where it started.

◀ These houses in San Francisco, USA, have been badly damaged by an earthquake. Though they were still standing when the photograph was taken, they would be quite unsafe to enter.

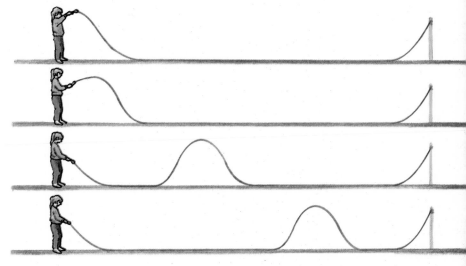

Inside the Earth

The deepest mines and boreholes go down only a few miles. So scientists have to use less direct methods to find out what our planet is like deep inside. Earthquake records tell us a lot. As earthquake waves pass through the Earth, they get altered by the material they go through. For example, S waves cannot pass through liquids, though P waves can. Only P waves are detected on the far side of the Earth from an earthquake, so part of the central region of the Earth must be liquid. By putting together all the clues in this way, the complete picture can be built up.

There are three main parts to the Earth: the *core*, the *mantle*, and the *crust*. The crust is the thin layer on which we live. It is made up of the lighter materials that, over millions of years, have worked their way to the surface from the underlying mantle and have gradually turned into rocks, soil, and sand.

▶ The Earth is made up of layers. Beneath the crust is the mantle. Then there is the dense liquid outer core. At the center is the solid inner core.

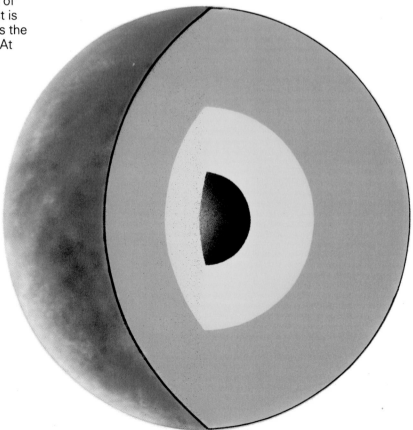

Because the crust is so thin, there are a few places where it has worn away completely to let the top of the mantle show through. This has happened in Cyprus and New Guinea, for example. The mantle is a dark, heavy rock. It is nearly the same all the way from the crust to the core, but its deeper layers are more compressed because of the weight above them. Below the mantle is the dense liquid outer core, probably made of molten iron, nickel, and a few other elements. The center of the Earth is very hot indeed – nearly as hot as the surface of the Sun. But the pressure is so great inside the Earth that the iron and other materials have solidified into a ball about 1,600 miles in diameter, called the inner core.

▲ Molten iron running down a channel. This is as near as we are likely to get to seeing what the deep interior of the Earth looks like.

▼ The Earth's mantle is made of a dull, dark, heavy rock called peridotite.

27

The future

What will happen to the Earth in the future? Scientists believe that, over the next 10,000 million years, continental movements and mountain-building will get slower, and earthquakes and volcanoes will get rarer. The processes of weathering, transportation, and deposition will still go on, though. The Earth will become flatter and duller, with no high mountains, and shallow oceans will cover most of the planet. But before the Earth ends up entirely covered by a shallow sea, something more dramatic will happen – the Sun will run short of the hydrogen it uses for fuel and become much larger than it is now. This will heat up the Earth, evaporating water from the seas and boiling the oceans dry. All life will be destroyed. Eventually the Sun will cool down, leaving the Earth as a dead, frozen planet.

We might make our planet uninhabitable long before any of this happens. For example, a large-scale

◄ Forests play an important part in keeping the atmosphere breathable. Burning them down could have very serious long-term effects.

nuclear war would make life on Earth impossible. Or we might increase the carbon dioxide in the atmosphere so that it forms a barrier that lets heat in but doesn't let it out. Carbon dioxide is produced by burning wood, coal, and gasoline and is soaked up by forests. So we must avoid burning too much fuel and cutting down too many trees. Another danger to our Earth is caused by the release of chemicals known as CFCs, which are used in refrigerators and aerosol sprays. These rise into the atmosphere and damage the ozone layer, which protects us from harmful radiation from the Sun. Fortunately, a lot of people recognize these dangers and are working to protect our planet. Our Earth is a delicate and beautiful planet, so we must take good care of it. It is all we have.

▲ The Yosemite National Park in California, USA. Surely no one would wish to take the chance of turning beautiful places such as this into uninhabitable deserts.

◀ Is this what the Earth will look like in its old age? No mountains, no deep oceans, just mile after mile of flat marshland and shallow seas.

Fact file

The Earth's orbit

The Earth's distance from the Sun varies between 91½ million miles in January and 94½ million miles in July. It takes one year, or 365¼ days, or 31½ million seconds, to complete its 590 million mile orbit. The Earth travels around the Sun at an average speed of about 67,000 miles per hour, or 19 miles per second.

Velocities

The Earth rotates once a day. Because of this rotation, a point on the equator is moving at 1,030 miles per hour, or 0.29 miles per second. Orbital velocity (the speed needed to launch a satellite into a circular orbit just above the Earth's surface) is 16 times as fast as this – nearly 5 miles per second. Escape velocity (the speed needed to escape from the Earth's gravity) is 7 miles per second.

The Earth's surface

The surface area of the Earth is nearly 197 million square miles. About 71 per cent of the surface is covered by water. This leaves an average of 7 acres of dry land for each one of the 5,000 million people estimated to live on Earth.

Life

All life known to exist in the universe is confined within the 10-mile thick layer at the surface of the Earth, except when there is an astronaut in orbit. Invertebrate animals (those with no backbones) are found throughout the whole of this height range, from crabs at the bottom of the oceans to small spiders found high on Mount Everest. Vertebrate animals (those with backbones, including fish, birds, and human beings) are found within a height-range of about 9 miles. Plant life is confined to a range of about 5 miles. Between 2 and 10 million different kinds of plants and animals are alive on Earth today.

Water

The biggest ocean is the Pacific, with a surface area of about 64 million square miles. The largest lake is the Caspian Sea, at 143,630 square miles. The deepest part of the ocean is the Mariana Trench in the Pacific Ocean, which is about 7 miles deep. From the top of Mount Everest to the bottom of the deepest ocean is less than one three-hundredth of the distance to the center of the Earth.

▼ The Atlantic Ocean pounds the coast of Galicia, in northwest Spain. This is one of the processes that changes the Earth's landscape.

Earthquakes

The strength of an earthquake is measured by its magnitude, expressed on the Richter scale in numbers from 0 to over 8. The approximate strength and number of earthquakes that occur each year is:

magnitude	number
3-3.9	49,000
4-4.9	6,200
5-5.9	800
6-6.9	108
7-7.7	17
7.8-8.6	2

Possibly the most violent earthquake ever was in Lisbon, Portugal, in 1755. About 60,000 people were killed, and the shock was felt up to 350 miles away.

▼ The eroded hills of Zabriskie Point, in Death Valley, California, USA.

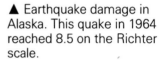

▲ Earthquake damage in Alaska. This quake in 1964 reached 8.5 on the Richter scale.

Hottest, coldest, wettest, driest

The hottest place on Earth is near its center, but the temperature on the surface varies from a maximum of 134°F recorded in Death Valley, California, USA, to a minimum of −129°F in Antarctica. Tutunendo, Colombia, has the most rainfall, averaging 463 inches each year, while the Sahara Desert averages less than 1 inch each year.

Volcanoes

There are about 500 active volcanoes and many more extinct ones. Some volcanoes, such as Stromboli in Italy and those found in Hawaii, erupt nearly all the time. The worst eruption ever recorded was on Krakatoa, in Indonesia, in 1883. The explosion was heard 2,900 miles away. The 115-foot high waves produced by the explosion flooded the shores of Java and Sumatra, killing 36,000 people. Ash was thrown so high into the atmosphere that it spread around the world.

31

Index